LORD OF THE FLIES

by
William Golding

Teacher Guide

Written by
Linda Herman

Note

The 2006 Perigee paperback edition of the novel, © 1954 by William Golding, was used to prepare this guide. The page references may differ in other editions. Novel ISBN: 978-0-399-50148-7

Please note: This novel deals with sensitive, mature issues. Parts may contain profanity and/or descriptions of violence. Please assess the appropriateness of this novel for the age level and maturity of your students prior to reading and discussing it with them.

ISBN 978-1-56137-383-3

To order, contact your local school supply store, or—

Novel Units, Inc.
P.O. Box 97
Bulverde, TX 78163-0097

Web site: novelunits.com

Table of Contents

Skills and Strategies

Comprehension
Identifying attributes, inferences, cause/effect, summarizing, decision-making, plot development

Literary Elements
Character analysis, setting, story mapping, conflict, theme, author's purpose, point of view, figurative language

Listening/Speaking
Discussion, presentation, dramatization

Writing
Personal narrative, dialogue, journalism, poetry, essay, report, pamphlet

Critical Thinking
Predicting, brainstorming, compare/contrast, analysis, evaluation, research

Across the Curriculum
Literature—*The Coral Island*; Social Studies—history, government, indigenous masks and dances, Dartmoor, philosophy; Health—children's fears, denial, post-traumatic stress disorder; Music—analysis, composition; Art/Media—illustration, map, collage, documentary

Genre: adventure, young-adult fiction

Setting: unknown Pacific island during a nuclear world war

Point of View: third-person omniscient

Themes: human nature, civilization, savagery, spirituality, identity, loss of innocence, evil, fear, domination, leadership, warfare, nature

Conflict: person vs. person, person vs. nature, person vs. society, person vs. self

Style: narrative, allegory

Tone: serious, apprehensive, tragic, violent

Date of First Publication: 1954

Summary

When an airplane carrying a group of British schoolboys crashes on a deserted island, the boys are stranded without adult supervision. They establish a society by electing 12-year-old Ralph as chief. Ralph, with assistance from the intelligent but annoying Piggy, prioritizes the survivors' needs—most importantly, a signal fire for rescue. Ralph appoints Jack as leader of the hunters, unaware that hunting will become Jack's savage obsession. Ralph's frustrations mount as fear spreads among the group and Jack challenges Ralph's authority. Jack's hunting skills and promises of fun entice most of the boys to leave Ralph's group and join Jack's tribe of war-painted, bloodthirsty hunters. Jack sets up a well-defended fort at the Castle Rock and then raids Ralph's group to steal Piggy's glasses, which are needed to start fires. After a failed attempt at retrieving Piggy's glasses, Ralph flees into the forest. Jack's tribe sets fire to the forest, forcing Ralph to run onto the beach, where he finds a naval officer who was alerted to the boys' presence by smoke from the forest fire. Ralph weeps for the loss of innocence and the darkness in man, causing the other boys to cry, too.

About the Author

William Golding was born in 1911 in Cornwall, England and began writing at the age of seven. Golding studied natural sciences at Brasenose College at Oxford for two years before transferring to an English literature program. In 1934, he received a B.A. in English and published his first book, *Poems*, before becoming a teacher. In 1937, Golding completed his post-graduate studies in education and then taught English and philosophy at Bishop Wordsworth's School in Salisbury until he joined the Royal Navy during World War II. After Golding left the navy, he returned to teaching until 1962, when he became a full-time writer. Best known for his first published novel, *Lord of the Flies* (1954), Golding also wrote plays, essays, short stories, poetry, a travel book about Egypt, and other novels such as *The Inheritors* (1955), *Pincher Martin* (1956), and *The Double Tongue* (1995), which was published posthumously. *Rites of Passage* (1980), the first novel in Golding's Sea Trilogy, won the Booker Prize. His novels are often allegorical with a theme of good versus evil. When Golding died in 1993, he left behind daily journals consisting of more than two million words. Golding was awarded the Nobel Prize for Literature in 1983 and was knighted in 1988.

Background Information

The following information will enhance students' understanding of the novel.

1. Influences: After years of studying science, Golding rejected his father's belief of rationalism, the theory that humanity is capable of perfection. Instead, Golding believed humanity is just as capable of evil as perfection and needs the structure of a democratic civilization to suppress its base instincts. The death and violence Golding saw during his service in the Royal Navy confirmed to him that the potential for evil resides within every human, and the political climate of the Cold War era reinforced his beliefs. In *Lord of the Flies*, Golding's beliefs are represented through a group of civilized British schoolboys who, without the structure of authority, resort to primitive behavior (e.g., following the strongest leader, committing murder) in order to survive and endure the horror of their situation. In a publicity questionnaire, Golding described the theme of the novel as "an attempt to trace the defects of society back to the defects of human nature. The moral is that the shape of a society must depend on the ethical nature of the individual and not on any political system however apparently logical or respectable."

   According to Golding, theater (especially Greek classics and Shakespeare) influenced his writing more than contemporary novelists. However, *Lord of the Flies* intentionally challenges unrealistic children's adventure stories, most notably R. M. Ballantyne's *The Coral Island* (1857). Both novels share similar plots and character names, though in *The Coral Island* the British boys remain innocent and noble during their island adventure, whereas the boys from *Lord of the Flies* resort to barbarism.

2. Allegory: Originally titled *Strangers from Within*, *Lord of the Flies* is an allegorical novel. Though it can be read as an adventure story, the novel is rich with symbolism, allusions, and hidden depth, all of which Golding uses to explore humans' inherent evil. The island is a microcosm of the world, with the characters representing various aspects of human nature. The characters' struggle to survive alludes to human evolution beginning with the creation of fire and ending with the collapse of society.

   As a political allegory, the characters' society reflects real-life society at the time the author wrote the novel. At the end of World War II, the world was divided into the free world and the Soviet Union, just as Ralph's and Jack's tribes are. Ralph's group symbolizes democracy, and Jack's tribe symbolizes a military dictatorship. Social classes are also represented with the older boys as political leaders and the younger boys as common people.

   Lord of the Flies is also a Freudian psychological allegory, which is based on the different sides of human personalities: the id, the superego, and the ego. Jack represents the id, the part of the mind that works to satisfy its own desires. Piggy represents the superego, which tries to control the impulsiveness of the id and make the ego act morally. Ralph represents the ego, which works to balance the demands of the id and the superego.

   With its biblical parallels, the novel is also a religious allegory. The island, like the Garden of Eden, is paradise until it is corrupted by the boys' inner evil. The evil is elicited by the boys' fear of the unknown creature they hear about. They refer to the creature as "Lord of the Flies" or "the beast," which are names also used to refer to Satan in many religions. The boys' descent into savagery mirrors the original fall of man. Simon, the mystic or visionary character, is often considered Christ-like. Simon feeds the younger boys, seeks the truth, is killed while spreading the truth, and has a name of biblical origin. The scene between Simon and the Lord of the Flies parallels the devil tempting Jesus during his 40 days in the wilderness. However, Simon's death does not bring salvation to the boys—rather, it causes more death and violence.

Characters

Ralph: 12-year-old protagonist; represents democracy and the civilized side of human nature; fair-haired, attractive, and athletic; elected leader of the boys by majority; a British naval commander's son

Piggy: Ralph's advisor; represents the scientific and rational side of human nature; short, overweight, and nearsighted; asthmatic; intelligent and socially awkward, making him vulnerable to the other boys; focuses on acting civilized

Jack Merridew: antagonist; represents the darker side of human nature with a desire for power and savagery; tall, thin, and bony with red hair and expressive blue eyes; uses military tactics to control the choir boys/hunters; obsessed with hunting and becoming chief

Simon: represents the spiritual side of human nature; skinny with coarse black hair; has fainting spells; shy, kind, and helpful, yet odd; searches for and faces life's truths; killed before sharing the truth about the beast

Sam and Eric ("Sam 'n Eric" or "Samneric"): identical twins; represent unity and the human need for moral support; stocky boys with golden-colored hair; inseparable; loyal to Ralph until forced to betray him

Roger: Jack's loyal follower; represents evil and humans' ability to harm others; slender, secretive, and sadistic; murders Piggy

"biguns": largest and oldest boys

Maurice: bigun; supports Jack

Robert: bigun; plays the part of the pig during the hunting ceremony

"littluns": smallest and youngest boys; represent the common people; view Ralph as an adult figure; spend days playing and nights fearing the beast

littlun with birthmark on his face: first to mention the beast; most likely killed in the wildfire

Henry: largest of the littluns; demonstrates domineering traits

Percival Wemys Madison: one of the smallest boys; indicator of the boys' declining civilized nature; suggests the beast lives in the sea; forgets his home address and later his name

Johnny: one of the smallest boys; well-built with fine hair; aggressive in nature

Bill, Harold, Phil, Wilfred, Stanley: other children stranded on the island

the beast: dead parachutist; represents the adults' warring civilization off the island

the Lord of the Flies: a pig's head impaled on a stick; symbolizes evil; Jack's offering to the beast; speaks to Simon and reveals the truth about the beast to him

naval officer: led to the island by Jack's forest fire; hypocritically chastises the boys for acting uncivilized

Initiating Activities

Use one or more of the following to introduce the novel.

1. As a class, discuss human nature: what is learned and what is instinctive? Read the back cover of the novel aloud, and then brainstorm about what type of "darkness" the novel might explore. Have students complete the "I Predict…" activity on page 28 of this guide.

2. Discuss Sigmund Freud's theory that the human psyche can be divided into three parts: id, ego, and superego. Have students create an artistic impression depicting the theory.

3. Have students research the Cold War and prepare a time line beginning with the ending of World War II. While researching, students should note the effects the Cold War had on the world's state of mind and consider William Golding's mindset as he wrote the novel in the early 1950s.

4. Ask students to volunteer definitions of the word "allegory." Then, explain to students that *Lord of the Flies* is an allegory. Students should determine the symbolism and the author's messages throughout the novel by completing an Allegory chart (see page 29 of this guide) for each chapter read.

5. Have students research British culture and traditions and discuss their findings in class. Students should keep a glossary of British-related vocabulary in the novel, providing definitions and citing page numbers. Examples of vocabulary words include: Home Counties, waxy, smashing, dazzle paint, bloody, and jolly.

Chapters One–Two

After their plane crashes, Ralph and Piggy clamber through the jungle toward a lagoon. Ralph, confident of eventual rescue by his naval commander father, thrills at freedom from adult supervision. Piggy, however, worries that no one will know their whereabouts since the atom bomb exploded after they evacuated Britain, likely killing everyone. Ralph and Piggy find a conch shell and use it to summon other survivors, including a group of choir boys led by Jack Merridew. The boys elect Ralph as their leader, and he names Jack as leader of the hunters. While exploring, Ralph, Jack, and Simon discover a wild pig, but Jack cannot bring himself to kill it. A small boy with a prominent birthmark claims to have seen a snake-like "beastie" in the jungle and is scoffed at by the older boys. The boys accidentally start a wildfire in their enthusiasm to build a signal to attract passing ships. Piggy points out that the boy with the birthmark is missing.

Vocabulary
effulgence
enmity
interposed
strident
furtive
suffusion
pallor
indignation
immured
hiatus
gesticulated
ebullience
grotesque
officious
recrimination
realism
tumult
tirade

Discussion Questions

1. Discuss the opening pages of the novel. What information is given about Ralph and Piggy's situation? What can you infer? *(An attack on a plane evacuating British schoolboys forces a crash landing that kills the pilot and the man with a megaphone. Ralph, confident that his naval commander father will rescue him, is delighted at the freedom from adults. He proceeds to play and swim naked. Piggy, who speaks of his aunt in the past tense, fears an atomic bomb has killed everyone who might have known where they are. Believing they may be stranded on the island forever, Piggy wants to find a resolution to their problem. Answers will vary, but students can infer that England is involved in a country-wide [or even worldwide] nuclear war.)*

2. Compare and contrast Ralph and Piggy. What do you learn about each boy from their interactions? *(Ralph is a fair-haired, attractive, confident, athletic boy, whose father is a commander in the Navy. Piggy, who is overweight, wears thick glasses, and has physical limitations due to his asthma, is intelligent and believes in acting properly. He is an orphan who was raised by his aunt and, based on his speech, is from a lower-class family. Ralph does not "need" Piggy; he slips away whenever Piggy becomes sick after eating the island's fruit, and he makes fun of the overweight boy's nickname. Piggy, however, craves friendship. He even trusts Ralph with his humiliating nickname and urges Ralph to assume the leadership role despite Piggy's intelligence. Piggy understands they're in danger, while Ralph wants to explore and have fun. Piggy demonstrates more maturity than Ralph; however, Piggy is whiny and seems delicate.)*

3. What is the significance of the setting? Based on the description of the island, do you expect the story to be a tropical adventure or a harrowing survival tale? Why? *(The island is a microcosm of the real world, which provides an opportunity to study human nature. The boys' isolation from civilization raises the questions: Will the boys choose to organize a civilized society, or will they become primeval? Do people need societal rules to curb savage tendencies? What of human nature is learned versus instinctual? Answers will vary, but students should mention that the setting becomes its own character in the novel and has a dual nature [much like humans do]. Palm trees, white surf, and bright, beautiful beaches imply a paradise offering an adventure; however, phrases*

such as "the darkness of the forest," "skull-like coconuts" [p. 10], and water "warmer than [Ralph's] blood" [p. 12], combined with the boys' sickness from the native fruit, foreshadow serious danger. The setting also alludes to the Bible's Garden of Eden and foreshadows a similar fate.)

4. Describe Jack's behavior when he encounters Ralph and Piggy. Regarding Jack and the choir boys, what might the metaphor, "The creature was a party of boys" (p. 19), foreshadow? *(Jack commands the choir boys as if they are a military unit. He arrogantly disrupts Ralph's meeting by asking the whereabouts of the adults and insulting Piggy. Then he insists he should be chief and simmers with anger once he can't find any adults. Answers will vary. The metaphor foreshadows Jack's evil nature and "the creature" that Jack and his obedient followers become.)*

5. Discuss Ralph's and Jack's leadership techniques. Is Ralph the best choice as leader? Do you think children can organize and maintain a successful society without adults? *(Ralph's leadership techniques are based on the democracy of England, while Jack leads through intimidation, much like a dictator. Ralph includes the other boys in decision-making, takes time to plan his actions, and shares power, as demonstrated by his giving Jack control over the hunters. Answers will vary. Jack has experience leading the choir, but he obviously desires more power for himself. Ralph is elected because of his calmness, size, attractive appearance, and possession of the conch. Students should consider that the boys' attempt to create a new society derives from a limited understanding of government and probably has little chance of succeeding.)*

6. How are similarities and differences in Ralph's, Jack's, and Simon's personalities revealed during the boys' exploration of the island? What is significant about the boys shoving the rock off the mountaintop? *(Answers will vary. The boys form friendships with each other as they childishly play around, unconcerned about survival. They discover a track through the jungle, which Ralph guesses was made by a person and Jack claims was made by animals; their choices foreshadow what each boy will eventually represent. At the top of the mountain, the boys savor feelings of domination, and Ralph asserts his authority as leader by claiming the island as theirs. Simon observes the details of nature, noting that the bushes look like candles, which implies he is capable of making connections between things that the other two boys cannot. Ralph's practicality leads him to point out that the buds cannot be lit, and Jack dismisses the plant because it is not edible. [Readers familiar with R. M. Ballantyne's* The Coral Island *will note that the boys stranded on the island in that novel knew they could use nuts from the candle tree to make candles.] Shoving the rock off the mountain is a childish challenge the boys cannot resist. Afterwards, they feel triumphant, not considering the possible damage done to nature on a whim.)*

7. What is the real reason Jack does not kill the piglet? Do you believe next time will be different? *(Jack has never killed anything before, so he hesitates "because of the enormity of the knife descending and cutting into living flesh; because of the unbearable blood" [p. 31]. Jack still shows civility, but his savagery is emerging. Angrily looking around, he thinks, "Next time there would be no mercy" [p. 31]. Answers will vary, but students might suggest Jack will stay true to his word because of his pride and the anger he shows afterward. He probably feels like he has failed and must redeem himself.)*

8. What does the conch symbolize? *(The conch initially represents communication since Ralph uses the shell to summon other survivors. It then becomes a symbol of authority, which allows the person holding it to speak. The conch is the first step toward the formation of a society and comforts the younger boys who need the stability of their home life. The conch symbolizes the order of society.)*

9. Why does Ralph repeatedly say there is not a beast on the island? What is the meaning of the statement "[Ralph] felt himself facing something ungraspable" (p. 37)? Is the beast real? *(Ralph and the older boys know the small island could not support a large beast, but the younger boys are not convinced. Answers will vary. Ralph is trying to convince himself that the beast does*

not exist because the "ungraspable something" that he senses comes from inside. The younger boys' imagined fears of the jungle create the beast. However, the beast is not an animal but the darker, aggressive side of human nature.)

10. Discuss the events surrounding the fire. How is the fire important to the novel? *(Ralph suggests building a fire to signal any passing ships. However, the boys allow their emotions to override rationality. They rush up the mountain "like a crowd of kids" [p. 38], tear off Piggy's glasses, and start a fire that is too big to control. "Life became a race with the fire" [p. 41] foreshadows Ralph's fleeing another fire at the end of the novel, and "On one side the air was cool, but on the other the fire thrust out a savage arm of heat that crinkled hair on the instant" [p. 41] describes the dual nature of the fire. The boys' intentions to build the fire are positive—they want to signal for help; however, the results of the fire are negative since the boy with the birthmark on his face has possibly died in the fire. The scene communicates how ambition can be good but being overly ambitious can have negative repercussions. Also, Jack's volunteering the hunters to keep the fire going indicates a slight shift in power between Ralph and Jack.)*

11. What does Piggy's relationship with the other boys indicate about human nature? *(Answers will vary. Piggy's relationship with the others is an example of how human nature often discriminates against the vulnerable. Since Piggy, with his health problems, is considered weak and needs civilization to protect him, the other boys pick on him to make themselves feel stronger and unified. Piggy annoys the other boys by trying to be responsible, which separates him further from them. Even though Piggy's suggestions make sense, the boys ignore him because they would rather have fun than act responsibly.)*

12. Why are names important to Piggy? What is the significance of Piggy's statement, "How could I [get a list of names] with them little 'uns running round like insects" (p. 46)? *(Answers will vary. Since the boys landed on the island, Piggy has been concerned with names. Ralph later instructs him to make a list of everyone's name. To Piggy, names are a product of civilization, a means of communicating and building a society. Ironically, Piggy never reveals his true name. His despised nickname links him to the island's pigs and foreshadows his fate. The quote explains why Piggy does not know how many kids there are, and it shows his frustration toward Ralph and the lack of order on the island. It may also be a play on the title, with the older boys being the "lords" and the younger boys the "flies.")*

Supplementary Activities

1. As you read the novel, add to the Clue Log on page 30 of this guide.

2. Write about a place (real or imagined) that delights you as much as the adult-free island delights Ralph.

3. Imagine you and your classmates are stranded on an island. Choose a leader, create a set of rules to follow, and assign certain tasks such as hunting or exploring to classmates. Explain your choices.

4. Research children's fear of monsters and ways to overcome such fears. Explain what Ralph does wrong while trying to alleviate the little boys' fear of the snake-like beast. Discuss how he should have handled the situation.

5. Keep a list of literary devices (such as metaphors, similes, and personification) as you read the novel, citing the page numbers on which you find them. Write one or two sentences explaining the significance of each literary device.

Chapters Three–Four

Jack becomes animal-like in his obsession with tracking pigs. Ralph's frustrations increase when no one but Simon helps build shelters. Henry expresses dominance and a desire for power, and Roger shows an interest in harming others by throwing stones close to Henry. A painted-on mask intended to provide camouflage allows Jack to break free from morality. Jack has Sam and Eric abandon their job maintaining the fire so they can go hunting with him. Jack and his hunters successfully slay a pig, but their victory celebration is marred when they return to find Ralph furious that the signal fire was out when a ship passed the island. Ralph scolds Jack for letting the fire go out. Jack becomes angry when he begins to feel blamed by everyone else and hits Piggy. Jack eventually apologizes, and the boys begin building the fire again. They cook and eat the pig, then Jack tells how they captured the pig. After the hunters stop chanting and dancing, Ralph calls a meeting.

Vocabulary
festooned
tendril
inscrutable
vicissitudes
compulsion
opaque
declivities
tacit
susurration
blatant
dubious
belligerence
chastisement
impalpable
detritus
preposterous
swarthiness
disinclination
implications
malevolently

Discussion Questions

1. What effect does hunting have on Jack? Do you think the island is changing Jack, or is Jack's true nature simply emerging? *(Jack is acting more like an animal as he learns how to track, creeping through the jungle on all fours with his nose inches from the ground and sniffing the air, "assessing the current of warm air for information" [p. 48]. Although Jack becomes afraid when he hears "a harsh cry" [p. 49] in the forest, his frustration and the thought of killing brings out his madness, and he becomes more determined to succeed in his hunt. Jack embraces his inner savage instincts and allows his civilized side to disappear while he hunts. Answers will vary. Some students might think Jack's true nature is surfacing since he eagerly accepts his role as hunter and is excited to kill. Other students may believe Jack is just doing what is necessary to survive and is trying to take care of the others.)*

2. Analyze the significance of the shelters. *(Answers will vary. According to Ralph, the shelters will protect the boys from rain and provide a home for the littluns, who need security to ease their terror-filled nights. The shelters represent the orderliness and discipline of home life in England. The shelters continuously falling down indicate that the boys' small society on the island is falling apart.)*

3. Why does Jack have difficulty expressing his feelings about hunting in the jungle? What do Simon's and Ralph's reactions imply? *(Answers will vary. Jack's inability to explain his feelings indicates he senses a change within himself but is reluctant to acknowledge it. He is probably starting to frighten himself and does not want the others to know his dark feelings. Simon's intentness implies he is not familiar with the feelings Jack is describing and that he is trying to understand Jack. Ralph may act indignant out of annoyance that Jack and the hunters are not helping to build shelters. Ralph may also feel skeptical because he senses the beast inside Jack but is unwilling to acknowledge the corrupt side of humans.)*

4. Explain the meaning of the following statement: "[Ralph and Jack] walked along, two continents of experience and feeling, unable to communicate" (p. 55). Do you think Ralph and Jack's relationship would change if they worked together? Do you agree with Ralph that building shelters is more important, or with Jack that they should be hunting for meat?

(Answers will vary. The statement suggests that Ralph's and Jack's priorities are as far apart as two continents and, just as continents support different cultures, Ralph and Jack don't think alike or have the same priorities. More importantly, neither boy attempts to understand the other's position. Some students may believe if Ralph and Jack communicated and worked together, they could accomplish much more. Others may believe that it is impossible for Jack and Ralph to work together because Jack's desire to kill is all-consuming.)

5. Discuss the significance of Simon's actions in the jungle when he walks off by himself. How does the author indicate that Simon symbolizes the goodness of man? *(Answers will vary. Simon is in harmony with nature, fully aware of the blooming candle-buds and the rhythm of the island. His secret place in the jungle is his sanctuary—somewhere he can go to meditate or find peace from the evil and fear around him. Simon depicts goodness and kindness when he picks the best fruit from the trees for the littluns since they cannot reach. He also takes time to appreciate the beauty of nature.)*

6. How are the littluns described, and how do they interact with the older boys? *(The littluns are the smaller, younger boys around the age of six, and they can easily be distinguished from the biguns. The littluns spend their days picking and eating fruit, from which they often suffer stomachaches and chronic diarrhea. They comfort each other when they have nightmares, and they do not cry for their mothers very much. The littluns also enjoy Ralph's meetings, and they consider Ralph an adult figure. They enjoy the simple fun of building sandcastles and usually stay away from the older boys.)*

7. Why do Maurice and Roger bully the littluns? How do Maurice's and Roger's actions signal that though they are becoming less civilized, societal norms still control their actions? *(Answers will vary. Maurice and Roger most likely bully the littluns because it is instinctual to pick on people weaker than themselves. However, Maurice and Roger show that they are still aware of societal rules when they pick on littluns. When Percival cries due to sand in his eye after Roger and Maurice kick the littluns' sandcastles over, Maurice feels guilty and runs away. He remembers being punished for the same offense some time ago, and "though there was no parent to let fall a heavy hand, Maurice still felt the unease of wrongdoing" [p. 60]. Roger struggles with the temptation to harm Henry but decides not to. Instead, Roger intentionally misses Henry when he throws the stones because there is an "invisible yet strong…taboo of the old life. Round [Henry] was the protection of parents and school and policemen and the law" [p. 62]. The "darker shadow [creeping] beneath the swarthiness of his skin" [p. 62] hints that evil is awakening inside.)*

8. Why does Jack paint his face? What happens as a result of wearing the mask? Why does the mask compel Sam and Eric to follow Jack? *(Jack intends the paint to camouflage him while hunting; however, the paint becomes a mask he hides behind and he feels "liberated from shame and self-consciousness" [p. 64]. He sheds the civility that has prevented him from acting upon his evil nature. Answers will vary. Though Sam and Eric are supposed to tend to the signal fire, the freedom from civilization that Jack obtains is contagious. The appearance of the mask has a power over the boys, so that they forget about responsibility and common sense and follow their desires.)*

9. What is the significance of Piggy being the only boy "whose hair never seemed to grow" (p. 64)? *(Answers will vary. Piggy's short hair seems to symbolize his remaining civility, since the other boys' shaggy, unkempt hair indicates their growing savagery. Piggy's short hair is also another element that ostracizes him from the other boys.)*

10. Why does Simon seem afraid when he looks between Ralph and the dead fire to the procession of returning hunters? What does the extinguished fire signify? *(Simon is a visionary who understands that the power struggle between Ralph and Jack is really a battle between civilization and savagery. He knows that Jack allowing the fire to die has caused irreparable damage, which will lead to the ultimate clash between Ralph and Jack and the good and evil that they*

represent. The fire is an indicator of the boys' link to civilization. If the fire permanently goes out, all hope of rescue is lost. For Jack, the fire is no longer important because he is more interested in hunting than being rescued.)

11. Discuss the significance of Jack hitting Piggy. *(Answers will vary. Jack is humiliated because he knows he is at fault for the fire going out and the ship passing them by. He is also angry with Ralph for not celebrating the successful hunt. Feeling that Piggy is beneath him, Jack loses his temper when Piggy blames him and some of the hunters join in. Jack's emotions are out of control and, though he earned the hunters' respect, he realizes they do not understand the savagery that motivates him. The breaking of Piggy's glasses symbolizes the loss of rationality, and this first act of physical violence against another hints at an increase of harm done to one another.)*

12. How does Ralph struggle to maintain leadership? How does Jack attempt to steal that leadership? *(Ralph stays calm and rational, refusing to participate in the hunters' celebration. He reminds Jack that he [Jack] allowed the fire to die. Though Ralph is unable to refuse the temptation of meat, he establishes control again by forcing the hunters to rebuild the fire in a different, less convenient location. Ralph waits for the hunters to finish their celebration dance and then calls an assembly in an attempt to restore order to the group. Jack intimidates Piggy and disrupts Ralph's plans by using the bloodlust of the hunt to appeal to the hunters' basic instincts.)*

13. Why do you think Ralph feels envious and resentful watching the hunters dancing and chanting? *(Answers will vary. Ralph likely feels this way because he has not had a moment of triumph like Jack with his successful hunt. Ralph probably resents the fact that he works hard to meet the group's needs without much help, while Jack does not follow their established rules and tempts the other boys to accompany him in his own endeavors.)*

Supplementary Activities
1. Write a poem that relates to Ralph's thought: "[Ralph] wanted to explain how people were never quite what you thought they were" (p. 54).

2. Research indigenous masks. Then, design a mask for Jack using colors found in nature.

3. Complete the Using Dialogue chart on page 31 of this guide.

4. Write an essay debating whether or not Jack was right to hunt instead of tend to the signal fire. Consider the consequences of his decision (e.g., the signal fire is out when a ship passes by).

5. Compare and contrast the democratic and totalitarian philosophies. Explain how Ralph's and Jack's actions and attitudes demonstrate these philosophies.

Chapters Five–Six

During the assembly, Ralph sternly reiterates the rules and addresses the littluns' fear of the beast. However, the solemn assembly turns chaotic when Percival begins to whimper and explain how the beast comes from the sea. Maurice offers ideas about what the beast could be, causing more arguing among the boys. Trying to make sense of "the beast," Simon suggests the beast is the boys themselves. When fear increases, Jack becomes angry and uses that anger to mask his and the other boys' fear. After the boys ignore Ralph and run off with Jack in an uproar, Ralph questions whether he should continue to be chief. While the boys sleep, an aerial battle takes place and a man parachutes onto the island (although he is dead before he hits the ground).

Sam and Eric see the wind-driven movements of the parachute and body from a distance and assume it is the beast. Ralph and the biguns set out to find the beast. The boys find nothing, and Ralph forces Jack and the others to return to the mountain to start the signal fire again.

Vocabulary
convulsion
ludicrous
derisive
effigy
lamentation
decorum
inarticulate
tempestuously
discursive
theorem
incantation
taut
interminable
tremulously
emphatic
embroiled
diffidently
plinth

Discussion Questions

1. What does it mean that Ralph finds himself "understanding the wearisomeness of this life, where every path was an improvisation and a considerable part of one's waking life was spent watching one's feet" (p. 76)? *(Answers will vary. Ralph expected to have fun and adventure on the island. Instead, he discovers primitive life is grueling work, especially weighed down with the responsibilities of leadership. Unlike Piggy, who does little work, or Simon, who ventures on his own to his secret place, Ralph does not have time for abstract thinking. When he needs to think, he takes a walk on the beach because it is the only place he does not have to watch where he steps. Ralph is losing his childish innocence, thinking more like an adult, and demonstrating his natural ability to lead.)*

2. What is the significance of the boys no longer obeying rules decided in their assemblies? How does fear contribute to the group's loss of happiness that they felt in the beginning? *(Answers will vary. Ignoring rules, such as not refilling the coconut shells with water and not using the designated rocks as a lavatory, indicates that the boys are becoming more primitive. They are satisfying personal desires rather than attending to the responsibilities necessary for rescue or a successful society. Fear, another primal human instinct, torments the littluns and even exists among the biguns. Fear weakens the boys' loyalty to Ralph. Though Ralph and Jack both declare there is no beast on the island, Jack's declaration carries more weight because he is the hunter. Unlike Ralph's logical approach, Jack's hunting skills and confidence offer protection and comfort to the frightened, desperate boys.)*

3. Why doesn't Piggy believe there is anything to fear? What is the importance of his exception, "Unless we get frightened of people" (p. 84)? *(Piggy explains that since life is scientific, rational explanations exist for everything. However, human nature is often unpredictable and confusing, so if the boys become scared of each other, danger may occur. Fear of people acknowledges that evil resides within humans and represents the boys' descent into savagery.)*

4. What is the significance of the scene with Percival? *(Answers will vary. Percival's hesitancy to speak reminds Ralph of the boy with the birthmark on his face who likely died in the fire. Percival's inability to recite his phone number indicates that his previous life is becoming a memory. When Percival begins to weep loudly because he is reminded of his home, the emotions of the other littluns are released as they are "reminded of their personal sorrows" [p. 87]. When Percival instantly falls asleep "surrounded by the comfortable presence of humans" [p. 88], he demonstrates how stressful life on the island is for the younger boys. Percival's fear that the beast comes from the sea also acknowledges the power and mysteries of the ocean.)*

5. Analyze the symbolism in the conflict between Ralph, Jack, and Piggy. *(Answers will vary. The conflict symbolizes the group's loss of control, the inevitable distance between them and "that understandable and lawful world" [p. 91]. Ralph, who represents government, depends on the rules.*

He states, "the rules are the only thing we've got!" [p. 91], meaning that society will break down without rules. Jack represents anarchy, or the lack of government. He openly rejects Ralph's authority as the elected chief and, as he breaks away from civilization, entices the other boys to follow. Piggy is the voice of reason, though the other boys always laugh at or ignore him.)

6. Do you think Ralph makes the right decision not to blow the conch to gather the boys again after they run off to find the beast? Should he give up leadership? *(Answers will vary. Some students may believe Ralph's inaction will cost him his leadership because his failure to keep order and control makes him appear weak. Others may feel Ralph's decision makes sense because the boys probably wouldn't have listened and would have just continued doing as they pleased. Blowing the conch would have made Ralph's lack of control more apparent. Students who think Ralph should remain chief may claim that any kind of civilization will be lost if he gives up because all this time he has kept Jack under control with rules. Without Ralph, Jack would probably be more savage and never try to get rescued. Students who think Ralph should give up being chief may claim that he is only fighting a losing battle and may as well not continue to stress himself.)*

7. Explain the irony of Ralph's, Piggy's, and Simon's confidence in adults. *(Answers will vary. The boys believe that if an adult were on the island, everything would be fine. They have confidence in adults because adults have always taken care of and protected them. Ironically, the boys think adults would not be quarreling as they are, yet they do not consider the nuclear war occurring off the island—between adults.)*

8. What does Simon consider to be "mankind's essential illness" (p. 89)? What do you think it means that "there rose before [Simon's] inward sight the picture of a human at once heroic and sick" (p. 103) when Simon thinks about the beast? *(Simon contends that the true beast is within the boys, that mankind's illness is the evil within every human. Once Simon determines that Sam and Eric's description of the beast defies logic, he pictures a human—amazingly wonderful yet marred by evil. Simon seems to be the only boy who understands the duality of human nature and what people are capable of.)*

9. Analyze the significance of "Something flitter[ing] there in front of [Ralph's] mind like a bat's wing, obscuring his idea" (pp. 107–108). *(As the other boys are pushing a rock over the cliff, Ralph realizes he is no longer focused on the fire—he forgot about rescue when he became concerned with hunting the beast in order to keep everyone safe. After he remembers the fire, he gets angry and immediately starts giving orders to Jack and the others to return to the mountain to relight the fire.)*

10. What role does fear play in Ralph's and Jack's struggles for leadership? *(Answers will vary. Fear highlights Ralph's and Jack's personalities and leadership skills under pressure. Ralph admits his fear, yet remains calm. He cares for the littluns, cautiously organizes a hunt for the beast, and acknowledges his responsibility as leader to explore the uncharted "castle" on his own. Jack, upon hearing of the beast on the mountaintop, wants to immediately kill it. He uses the fearful situation as an opportunity to take control of the group. He scoffs at Ralph and Piggy for being afraid, criticizes Simon, Bill, and Walter for their unhelpful comments, and announces that no one else should make decisions but the leaders. On the hunt, Jack mocks the others as he walks "with theatrical caution" [p. 103], although his own fears are revealed as he hesitates when Ralph offers him the opportunity to lead the way to the castle.)*

11. In relation to Ralph and Jack, examine the loyalty of the other boys. *(The boys' loyalty switches between Ralph and Jack. The boys still want to be rescued and return to civilization, though they do not want to focus on the fire and survival like Ralph. Jack's zeal for hunting the beast offers a target for the boys' fears and, in theory, a solution if they were to kill the beast. Having fun hunting with Jack and exploring the castle appeal to the boys, allowing them to temporarily forget their fears rather than address them, as Ralph would have them do.)*

Supplementary Activities

1. Consider Jack's statements about Ralph being elected chief: "Why should choosing make any difference? Just giving orders that don't make any sense—" (p. 91). Write one to two paragraphs discussing whether you think voters are obligated to follow elected leaders.

2. Create a "grownup sign" to guide Ralph as chief of the boys. Your sign may be artwork or a written message.

3. Sketch or paint the beast based on Sam and Eric's description found on page 100 of the novel. Compare and contrast your artwork with your classmates'. Discuss how some details come from the novel but also how the reader fills in details with his or her imagination.

4. Write a how-to article for a teen magazine about overcoming fear of public speaking.

Chapters Seven–Eight

On the boys' way to the mountain, Ralph wounds a boar and for the first time understands the thrill of hunting. Jack goads Ralph and Roger into climbing the mountain in the darkness. The boys find the dead parachutist at the top of the mountain and run away, thinking it is the beast. Jack calls an assembly and tries to persuade the boys to follow him rather than Ralph. When the boys do not support Jack, he becomes angry and embarrassed and abandons them to form his own group. Ralph and the others start a new fire on the beach. Jack and his tribe agree not to hunt the beast, but rather offer part of their kills to it as a sacrifice. They brutally slaughter a mother sow and leave her head on a stake as a gift to the beast. Simon witnesses the slaughter. Before fainting, Simon becomes deluded and imagines the pig's head (called "the Lord of the Flies") is talking to him. Jack and his hunters raid Ralph's tribe for fire.

Vocabulary
coverts
obtuseness
vulnerable
luxuriance
traverses
sagely
impervious
bravado
rebuke
demure
fervor
cynicism
obscene
illusive
runnels
vexed
parody

Discussion Questions

1. What can you infer from the following information: "[Ralph's fingernails] were bitten down to the quick though he could not remember when he had restarted this habit nor any time when he indulged it" (p. 109)? *(Answers will vary. Students will likely infer that the uncomfortable circumstances on the island make Ralph nervous. It is probably a habit he had when he was younger since he says, "Be sucking my thumb next—" [p. 109] after he realizes how much he has been biting his nails.)*

2. What does Ralph note about his appearance? Why does this concern him? *(Ralph seems disgusted with his lack of hygiene. He knows that he needs to wash his clothes, cut and wash his hair, take a bath, and brush his teeth. Yet he also lacks the motivation to do any of these things, even if he could. Ralph admits to this lack of motivation, and this is what concerns him the most—the knowledge that he has stopped caring about his appearance other than a casual observation of what should be done to improve it. He notes the disheveled appearances of the other boys, but he realizes "with a little fall of the heart that these were the conditions he took as normal now and that he did not mind" [p. 110].)*

3. Why can't Ralph dream of rescue while he is on the other side of the island? *(On the lagoon side of the island, Ralph can envision rescue because mirages hide the vastness of the ocean. But the other side of the island does not have mirages, and Ralph suddenly feels helpless. Faced with the enormous ocean separating him from civilization, Ralph feels rescue is impossible.)*

4. What is significant about Simon telling Ralph, "You'll get back to where you came from" (p. 111)? *(Answers will vary. Simon appears to read Ralph's mind. He watches Ralph closely and notes his body language, determining what Ralph is feeling. Some students might even think Simon stating "Ralph" alone will get home foreshadows his [Simon's] fate.)*

5. Why does Ralph change his opinion about hunting? What is the importance of the scene in which the boys reenact the hunt? *(Ralph gets excited after he wounds a boar. He enjoys the respect shown to him by the other hunters and decides hunting is good. When the hunters reenact Ralph's attack, Ralph experiences the desire to hurt Robert, who is pretending to be the pig. The scene shows that Ralph is capable of violence; the story's hero, like all humans, has a dark side. The scene continues with Robert pointing out that in order to complete the ceremonial dance, a real pig must be killed. His statement demonstrates how important killing has become to some of the boys. Jack takes Robert's statement further by suggesting they substitute a littlun for the pig. To Jack, the littluns are worthless, and his remark signifies that the level of his savagery has escalated to where he is now capable of killing a human.)*

6. Why might the author have included the detailed description of the boys' journey to the mountain on pages 116–117 of the novel? *(Answers will vary. The shift from short paragraphs with a lot of dialogue to one long paragraph with more complex sentence structure changes the mood. The paragraph mirrors Ralph's dreamy state as he continues to struggle through the tangled jungle.)*

7. Why does Ralph conclude that Jack hates him? Why do the rest of the boys on the journey become uneasy when Ralph confronts Jack, "as though something indecent had been said" (p. 118)? *(Ralph realizes that Jack always becomes antagonistic and challenges him when Ralph assumes leadership of the boys. When Ralph takes responsibility, Jack attempts to make him look foolish in front of the others. The boys sense the coming argument between Ralph and Jack. Because they respect Ralph and fear Jack, the boys become uneasy.)*

8. Analyze the effects of Ralph's agreement to climb the mountain in the dark. *(Answers will vary. Ralph's sense of rationality tells him to wait for daylight before hunting the beast; however, he wants to appear strong and brave in front of the other boys so he climbs the mountain. By allowing Jack to goad him into climbing the mountain in the dark, Ralph's authority weakens and Jack's power strengthens in the boys' perspective. If Ralph had waited until morning, the boys would have recognized the ape-like creature as a dead parachutist. Instead, the "beast's" existence is confirmed. Students should note that the author's imagery emphasizes the boys reverting to primitive instincts. Ralph "fus[ing] his fear and loathing into a hatred" [p. 123] implies he found courage through primitive instincts. The boys' fight-or-flight instincts send them fleeing from the beast. Ralph describes Jack and Roger as "creatures crying out and leaping" [p. 123].)*

9. Explain the significance of Jack's statement: "I'm not going to play any longer. Not with you" (p. 127). *(Jack, humiliated that the other boys still want Ralph as chief, decides to leave the group. His childish declaration reminds readers that Jack is a young boy, which makes his transitioning into savagery more tragic. The statement also implies that Jack considers life on the island a game, not a matter of survival. It shows he is more concerned with obtaining power and favor than being rescued.)*

10. How does Piggy's attitude change after Jack leaves the group? *(Piggy relaxes and becomes more assertive once Jack leaves. He suggests building the fire on the beach, which gives Ralph and the other boys hope of rescue during the day and security at night. For once, Piggy gathers firewood and even lights the fire himself with his glasses. He gains confidence and becomes an active member of the group.)*

11. Why do many of the biguns refrain from ousting Ralph as chief but then sneak away to join Jack's group? *(Answers will vary. The boys know their best chance of rescue is keeping the signal fire lit; however, they would rather have fun with Jack and eat meat instead of only fruit. The boys choose to satisfy their personal desires and are ashamed to admit it.)*

12. Why do you think the author gives such a detailed description of the brutal slaughter of the sow? What does Jack's selection of the mother sow indicate? *(Answers will vary. The scene demonstrates that the boys no longer hunt only for the purpose of food; instead, they enjoy the dominance and pleasure of killing. The boys are becoming degenerate and are losing their last shred of decency. The brutal manner in which they kill the pig also shows the level of depravity they have descended to. The tribe's behavior toward the mother sow may also foreshadow Piggy's fate since, like Piggy, the mother sow is vulnerable. Jack may have chosen her in order to feel powerful since he had just been humiliated in front of the boys when he failed to overthrow Ralph as chief.)*

13. Explain the significance of staking the sow's head. *(Jack leaves the sow's head as a gift to appease the beast. The offering signifies that the boys now worship the beast and have found a way to control their fear. Jack uses fear of the beast and the sow's head as a way to gain power over the boys. Since the boys are so afraid and see Jack's confidence in his actions, they feel safe to follow his lead.)*

14. Discuss the scene in which Simon hallucinates about having a conversation with the Lord of the Flies. How does this scene support the novel's theme of evil? Explain why the scene can be interpreted as having religious connotations. *(Answers will vary. The staked sow's head, named the Lord of the Flies, symbolizes evil and confirms to Simon that evil comes from within each boy. The scene depicts confrontation between good and evil and establishes Simon as the representative of the spiritual side of human nature. "Lord of the Flies" is a translation of the Greek "Beelzebub," a devil—often called Satan in the Bible. The confrontation resembles the scene in the Bible where the devil tempts Jesus in the wilderness. Simon, like Jesus, does not succumb to evil. Note that the Lord of the Flies warns that Ralph and Piggy will help Jack's tribe kill Simon if he interferes with their fun. This may be interpreted as temptation and desire attacking morality and virtue.)*

Supplementary Activities
1. Write a poem about bravado.

2. Complete the Thought Bubble activity on page 32 of this guide, expressing Roger's thoughts about hunting with Ralph and Jack.

3. Write an essay explaining whether you would stay with Ralph or join Jack's group if you were stranded on the island with them.

4. Analyze the lyrics of the song "Lord of the Flies" by Iron Maiden, and relate it to events in the novel. Note: Teachers may want to limit online browsing to only this song.

Chapters Nine–Ten

Simon walks back up the mountain and discovers that "the beast" is the dead parachutist and harmless. He frees the parachutist's tethered lines and then returns to the beach to tell the others the truth about the beast. At Jack's feast, Ralph and Piggy join the tribe's frenzied dance. When Simon comes from the forest to tell the others about the beast, he stumbles into the boys' circle and they kill him, thinking he's the beast. Ralph, Piggy, Sam, and Eric feel remorse but deny their participation in Simon's death. At the Castle Rock, Jack tells his tribe they did not kill the beast. Jack, Maurice, and Roger raid Ralph's camp and steal Piggy's glasses.

Vocabulary
corpulent
succulent
sauntered
demented
superficial
complementary
abominable
phosphorescence
inquisitive
befouled
somberly
torrid
assimilating
interrogative
theological
purged

Discussion Questions

1. What might Simon's journey up the mountain parallel? *(Answers will vary. Arguments can be made that Simon is similar to Moses and other prophets, seeking truth and wanting to enlighten others. Simon's journey is suggestive of Moses bringing the Ten Commandments down the mountain.)*

2. What does the simile "like an ape" imply in the sentence, "Power lay in the brown swell of [Jack's] forearms: authority sat on his shoulder and chattered in his ear like an ape" (p. 150)? *(Answers will vary. The simile may refer to the evolution of humans descending from apes, or it may describe the animalism present within humans.)*

3. How does Jack gain control of the boys, and how does Ralph attempt to keep his power as chief? Do you think Ralph will be able to keep control of the boys? *(Jack rejects civilization and embraces tribal leadership. Appealing to the boys' primitive instincts with promises of fun and protection from the beast allows Jack to rule like a dictator, and the boys willingly follow his orders. Ralph attempts to maintain his power by reminding the boys that they voted him chief and they agreed to keep the signal fire going. He appeals to the boys' logical and civilized side but is ineffective. When Ralph points out that Jack foolishly has not provided shelter against the storm, Jack urges the boys to do their victory dance. He again diverts the boys' attention and channels their increasing nervous energy. Answers will vary. Students might infer that Ralph will lose his power over the boys since it seems Jack has already gained a lot of favor among them.)*

4. Why do Ralph and Piggy participate in the tribe's dance? *(The approaching storm frightens Ralph and Piggy, so they seek to become part of the group that is a "demented but partly secure society" [p. 152]. They feel safe and in control of their fears when they "touch the brown backs of the fence" [p. 152]. Ironically, rather than keep the beast away, the "fence" traps the beast inside the boys' circle.)*

5. What does Simon's death represent? What does the imagery surrounding Simon's death imply about good and evil? *(Simon's death represents savagery overtaking civilization. Ralph and Piggy [two of the few who have remained sensible] joining in the chaotic dance indicates how enticing barbarity has become. Not even Ralph or Piggy are able to acknowledge that it is not the beast, but Simon whom they are harming. The imagery of brightness, pearls, and silver reflect Simon's goodness, while the tide pulling his body out to sea implies that goodness has left the island.)*

6. What might the parachutist's body floating away from the island symbolize? *(Answers will vary. The parachutist came from the outside world. His departure may symbolize civilization abandoning the island.)*

7. Analyze how Ralph, Piggy, Sam, and Eric deal with Simon's death. How can their reactions be applied to the novel's theme of civilization versus savagery? *(Ralph admits to Piggy that he participated in Simon's death. Ralph feels loathing; however, there is a feverish excitement in his voice that implies an inner battle. Intellectual Piggy cannot make sense of the truth. He attempts to rationalize or dismiss the killing, even going so far as to place blame on Simon. Sam and Eric, who obviously had already agreed to hide their participation, provide Ralph and Piggy with an excuse. Participation in Simon's death demonstrates that savage instincts, or evil, also reside in civilized people, those who are intelligent and morally good. Ralph's group denying their participation implies there still remains some awareness of right and wrong.)*

8. How does Jack deal with Simon's death? Explain his motivations to keep the beast alive. *(Jack tells his tribe that Simon was really the beast in disguise. He says the tribe did not kill the beast. Jack needs to keep the beast alive in order to control the tribe. He uses the tribe's fear of the beast to unite the boys, force them to respect him as chief, and justify his violence. When it suits his needs, Jack also regards the beast as an idol.)*

9. What does Ralph's statement, "Let the fire go then, for tonight" (p. 164), signify? *(The fire now serves two purposes: a means of comfort and the only tool for rescue. Ralph suggesting to let the fire die implies the loss of hope. The boys' hope of rescue diminishes, as does their hope for order and normalcy on the island. Ralph and Piggy realize that they will lose their sanity and surrender to their primal instincts if they don't leave the island soon.)*

10. What does Jack stealing Piggy's glasses signify? *(Answers will vary. It signifies that hope has been lost because he stole Ralph's only way to make a signal fire for rescue and because it is likely that Jack has no intention of using fire for rescue. Jack attacks Ralph's civilization and steals the only scientific technology on the island, further strengthening his position as chief. Jack also leaves Piggy blind and vulnerable.)*

Supplementary Activities

1. Working in small groups, research indigenous tribal dances and their purposes. Then, choreograph your own dance. Choose a theme for your dance, and add appropriate music. If approved by your teacher, perform your dance for the class.

2. Write a paragraph analyzing how the author creates suspense in the scene of Simon's death.

3. Research denial as a defense mechanism. Then, write a letter to Ralph that encourages him to accept partial responsibility for Simon's death and to move forward in life.

4. Choose an interesting topic about Dartmoor in England (e.g., ponies, bogs, archaeology, legends), and create a one-page illustrated report about your topic.

Chapters Eleven–Twelve

Ralph, Piggy, Sam, and Eric travel to the Castle Rock to retrieve Piggy's glasses. Ralph and Jack fight, and the tribe restrains Sam and Eric. Roger releases a leveraged rock, shattering the conch and killing Piggy. Jack and his tribe attack Ralph, and he flees into the jungle. Ralph discovers that Sam and Eric were forced to join Jack's tribe. Sam and Eric warn Ralph about Jack's plan to hunt and kill him the next day. The tribe sets fire to the jungle and forces Ralph out onto the open beach, where he finds a British naval officer. The officer assumes the boys are playing war games and having adventures. After learning of the two deaths and seeing the boys' condition, he criticizes them for not acting like proper British boys. Ralph surrenders to grief and weeps for the end of innocence, the darkness inside man, and his friend Piggy, causing the other boys to cry also. The officer, embarrassed by the boys' show of emotion, looks away toward his ship.

Vocabulary
luminous
myopia
propitiatingly
vitality
quavered
truculently
anonymity
cessation
parried
talisman
inimical
ululation
ensconce
cordon
crepitation
excruciatingly
epaulettes
distended

Discussion Questions

1. Explain the significance of Ralph wanting himself, Piggy, Sam, and Eric to look well-groomed when they approach Jack for Piggy's glasses. *(Ralph believes looking like proper British boys will influence Jack to return Piggy's glasses. Ralph is trying to remain mature and calm because "after all [he and the other three boys] aren't savages really and being rescued isn't a game" [p. 170]. He believes he can reason with Jack by showing they are civil and non-threatening.)*

2. Why do the twins look at Ralph strangely when Piggy implies that Ralph has forgotten the purpose of a fire? *(Answers will vary. Ralph is having difficulties focusing his thoughts and remaining collected. Most likely, Sam and Eric are just noticing Ralph's weakness. They may be comparing Ralph's leadership abilities to Jack's strength.)*

3. How much influence does the conch have over Jack and his tribe? *(The tribe no longer respects the conch as a symbol of authority and civilization. However, they still respond to the conch call, perhaps out of habit or the vague hope of rescue. The boys assemble along the ledge when Ralph blows the conch and hesitate when Jack orders them to grab Sam and Eric, almost as if remembering Ralph is chief when holding the conch. The boys also fall silent when Piggy holds up the conch and demands the right to speak. After the conch shatters, Jack screams wildly that Ralph no longer has a tribe and that he [Jack] is now chief. Despite his previous claims, Jack still believes the conch represents authority. Jack does not truly feel in charge until the conch is destroyed.)*

4. Moments before his death, Piggy asks Jack's tribe, "Which is better—to be a pack of painted Indians like you are, or to be sensible like Ralph is...to have rules and agree, or to hunt and kill...law and rescue, or hunting and breaking things up" (p. 180)? Why do you think Piggy believes he can reason with Jack's tribe despite all that has happened? *(Answers will vary. Piggy relies on society's rules and holds on to them as tightly as he does the conch. He expects others to live by the same standards. Piggy assumes everyone thinks as he does and refuses to believe that the other boys have completely surrendered to their savage instincts.)*

5. How is Piggy's death significant? *(Answers will vary. Piggy's death symbolizes the loss of intelligence and reason on the island. By holding on to the conch, Piggy was holding on to the structured rules of civilization that he valued. The destruction of the conch symbolizes the loss of law and order. Ralph loses Piggy's intellectual advice and will now have to fight Jack alone. Students may also note that, while Simon's death could be viewed as an accident, Piggy's death was premeditated by Roger. Jack's tribe has finally sunk so low as to commit murder. It is now uncertain if the boys will ever be able to return from their descent into treachery.)*

6. Explain the meaning of "The hangman's horror clung round [Roger]" (p. 182). How does Roger's savagery differ from Jack's? *(Roger is being compared to a public executioner, and the "hangman's horror" is guilt that person might feel after an execution. Roger's savagery differs from Jack's because Roger actually enjoys hurting others. Jack is a tyrant and acts violently when he feels it is necessary—not just because he thinks it is fun.)*

7. Analyze Ralph's encounter with the Lord of the Flies. What can you infer from the scene? *(Answers will vary. Ralph does not know the story behind the staked sow's skull, but he senses its evilness and the message it gave to Simon: the beast is within the boys. His "sick fear and rage" [p. 185] implies that Ralph feels humanity's struggle between good and evil. The "skull that gleamed as white as ever the conch had done" [p. 185] indicates the skull is Jack's symbol and, as Roger destroyed Ralph's symbol [the conch], Ralph destroys the staked skull.)*

8. What do you think Sam and Eric mean when they say Roger has "sharpened a stick at both ends" (p. 190)? What are Jack and Roger planning to do to Ralph? Why do they want to do this? *(Answers will vary, but students will assume that Roger and Jack plan to behead Ralph and leave his head as a staked offering to the beast—just as they did with the mother sow. Jack most likely wants to kill Ralph because he views him as a threat to his [Jack's] total control of the island. Ralph is also the last symbol of humanity, and Jack wants barbarity to rule.)*

9. Analyze Ralph's thoughts preceding and during the hunt. How does he use both the civilized and savage sides of human nature during the hunt? *(Ralph determines that Jack will never stop hunting him. Despite the danger, Ralph stays close to the tribe because he still needs to be close to people to ward off his fears of the night. During the hunt, Ralph wishes he had more time to strategize. He misses Piggy's advice, the solemn debates during assemblies, and the dignity of the conch. Although Ralph is still civil and rational, his survival instincts dominate as he flees the tribe and he becomes more animalistic—hiding, panting, snarling, lunging, and "running with the swiftness of fear" [p. 195].)*

10. What is ironic about Jack's wildfire? *(Jack intends to kill Ralph by creating the wildfire, but instead the fire brings rescue. Also, it is Jack who saves the boys despite Ralph's diligence about keeping the signal fire lit.)*

11. A *deus ex machina* is the unexpected arrival of someone or something that provides a quick resolution in extreme difficulty. The British naval officer is a *deus ex machina*. Why do you think the author chose to end the story with this literary device? *(Answers will vary. Seeing the boys from the officer's point of view reminds readers that the main characters are young boys. No longer is Jack a savage tribal chief but "a little boy who [wears] the remains of an extraordinary black cap..." [p. 201]. The author also contrasts the officer with Ralph and Jack, perhaps asking readers to consider the fine line between civilization and savagery. The officer, like Ralph and Piggy, expects proper behavior from the boys. His comment that "...a pack of British boys...would have been able to put up a better show than that..." [pp. 201–202] reminds readers of Jack's earlier statement, "We're English, and the English are best at everything. So we've got to do the right things" [p. 42]. Ironically, the officer berates the boys for warring, yet the adult civilization is also at war. This irony is highlighted by the novel's last sentence where the officer turns away to look at his warship. The deus ex machina provides hope at the end of the story and leaves readers thinking about the novel's messages.)*

12. What is significant about Percival's inability to remember his name? *(Percival demonstrates how far removed the boys are from civilization. Earlier in the novel, Percival is able to introduce himself with his full name and home address but cannot remember his telephone number. This was a sign that he was already slipping away from society, but his inability to even remember his name shows just how far he has slipped. Disorder has replaced all knowledge of the boys' former lives in society.)*

13. Why does Ralph weep at the end of the novel when the officer saves them? *(Ralph weeps "for the end of innocence, the darkness of man's heart" [p. 202], and the loss of Piggy. Ralph's experiences on the island change him from being just a boy who is happy to be free from adult supervision to a much more mature boy who has witnessed death and now knows about the inherent evil within humans. Ralph's life, as well as those of the other boys, will never be the same.)*

Supplementary Activities

1. Write a dialogue that takes place between Ralph and Jack on the flight back to England.

2. Choose a character from the novel. Using a computer program, design a before and after illustration showing how your character looked when he arrived on the island and how he looks when the boys are rescued.

3. Rewrite Chapter Twelve, "Cry of the Hunters," from Jack's point of view.

4. Complete the "Think About It" chart on page 33 of this guide.

Post-reading Discussion Questions

1. Evaluate *Lord of the Flies* as an allegory. What might Ralph, Jack, and Piggy symbolize? *(Answers will vary. The novel explores human nature and its civilized and savage sides. The setting is a microcosm of the world that is filled with objects used as symbols, such as the conch—the symbol of civilization—and the Lord of the Flies—the symbol of evil. Ralph, Jack, and Piggy represent humanity with varying social classes. The boys' steps toward creating a civilized society with a leader, rules, the conch, and fire mirror the evolution of the human race. The power struggle between Ralph and Jack demonstrates the building conflict between the good and bad sides of humans. Ralph's and Jack's differing opinions represent the views of a variety of governments or countries. Each main character in the novel represents an aspect of human nature. Ralph, the elected leader, represents civilization and structure. Jack, the savage, represents anarchy as he disrupts Ralph's meeting and attempts to gain power for himself. Jack's growing desire to hunt symbolizes the primitive, evil nature of humans. Piggy, the scientific and rational individual, symbolizes the helplessness the other boys feel. He is the intellectual and moral conscience of civilization—a voice of reason. Piggy's glasses might represent clear-sightedness. Refer to the Background Information on page 4 of this guide for details regarding the political, psychological, and religious allegorical aspects of the novel.)*

2. Discuss the meaning of the title of the novel. Why do you think the author originally titled the novel *Strangers From Within*? *("Lord of the Flies" has several meanings, both literal and symbolic. Literally, the title is the name of the staked sow's head—the bloody, decaying object that attracts swarms of flies. The staked head becomes Jack's symbol of power and an idol to worship. However, "Lord of the Flies" is also the translation of Beelzebub, another name for Satan. Symbolically, the title means evil and, as the staked head told Simon, the evil resides within each boy. Answers will vary, but students should infer that the "strangers from within" are the boys' evil or savage natures.)*

3. How is fear important to the story? *(Answers will vary. The novel addresses fear on an individual level, a group level, and as a defect of human nature. As individuals, humans fear the unknown and it is the littluns' fear of the unknown that creates the beast. This fear leads to irrational behavior, such as Sam and Eric's exaggerated reports of the beast chasing them down the mountain. Fear also creates myths or superstitions that attempt to explain the unknown, as shown by the group's rationalizations ranging from sea monsters to ghosts. At a group level, fear becomes infectious and leads to mob mentality. Once the older boys believe in the beast's existence, fear spreads and most of the boys turn to Jack for protection. Jack uses the boys' fear to divide the group, make himself more powerful, and manipulate his tribe. He presents the beast as an idol that needs sacrifices, says the beast can disguise itself, and claims the beast cannot be killed. Though fear never overrides Piggy's common sense, only Simon realizes the truth, that the beast the boys fear comes from within—the boys fear their own capabilities for violence. As a theme in the novel, fear is shown as a defect in human nature that must be overcome to find wisdom. The boys, however, do not unite to overcome their fears. Instead, they succumb to their fears and become enemies.)*

4. What does the novel suggest about society and human nature? *(Answers will vary. It can be gathered from the novel that humans left to rule themselves can be selfish and violent. The novel proves how humans need society, despite its flaws and conflicts, in order to restrain their basic instincts. However, a society's leaders greatly affect its functionality. Ralph bases his leadership on survival and the good of the group, yet he loses control to Jack, who plays on the boys' fears and promises fun, freedom from rules, and protection. If leadership fails, or if too great a number of individuals succumb to their base desires, the resulting evil can break down society. With Jack in charge, savagery reigns and Ralph's society fails. Ralph, Piggy, and Simon recognize their inherent*

evil but do not completely surrender to it, while Jack and Roger [who are only interested in self-gratification] turn cruel. Though every human is capable of barbarism, individuals can restrain themselves to varying degrees, especially with the law and order of society. A society with strong, ethical leaders can help less restrained individuals remain civilized. For example, even Roger controls his sadistic nature when throwing rocks near Henry. Roger only breaks free from society's restraints under Jack's leadership. The novel also implies that facing one's inner beast provides the only hope for humankind.)

5. What does the novel indicate about human relationships with nature? *(Answers will vary. From the beginning, the boys do not show respect for nature and their arrival on the island is like an invasion. The boys lose control of a destructive wildfire, topple boulders for fun without regard for the resulting damage, and are careless about sanitation practices. How the boys deal with the island wilderness represents humans' relationships with nature. Only Simon is in complete harmony with nature. Ralph, aware of the island's beauty and its dangers, prefers civilization. Jack seeks to dominate nature by hunting its creatures and setting a fire that destroys all life forms in it. The boys ultimately leave the pristine island in ruins.)*

6. How would the novel be different if the boys had initially elected Jack as chief? *(Answers will vary. Some students will feel that Jack may have immediately turned the group into a tribe and his savagery may have infected the boys sooner. Others may believe that having the power he craved would have satisfied Jack and prevented him from developing his obsession with hunting and killing. With sole responsibility of the group's survival, Jack may have used leadership skills appropriate for a civilized British boy.)*

7. Analyze the shift in references to Jack beginning in Chapter Ten. What might this represent? *(Following Simon's death, specifically beginning on page 159 of the novel, Jack is not mentioned by name among his tribe. The narrator also does not use his given name when describing scenes involving only Jack and his tribe. He is referred to only as "the chief" during these moments in the story. Any time Ralph or members of his group are present, Jack is once again referred to by name. Answers will vary. Students should infer that after Simon's death, Jack's tribe finally succumbs completely to their primitive sides. Any trace of kindness, gentleness, or awareness of proper behavior is lost, and they know only what "the chief" instructs them to do. As the leader of the savages, Jack has lost all aspects of his humanity and is never again known by the name given to him before landing on the island—breaking his final connection to the outside world. Ralph and his group are not yet entirely devoid of goodness, so they still recognize Jack as the boy he once was [although they are aware of the changes within him].)*

8. Review the major symbols discussed while reading the novel. Does any of the symbolism change during the story? Can you identify other symbols in the novel? *(Answers will vary. Major symbols include the conch, Piggy's glasses, the signal fire, the beast, and the Lord of the Flies. The conch symbolizes authority, civilization, law and order, and a democratic government with freedom of speech. However, the conch gradually loses its power and its destruction symbolizes the end of civilization and rational behavior on the island. Piggy's glasses symbolize knowledge, science, and perception. Without Piggy's glasses, the boys cannot start a fire. Since the glasses also represent intellect, Ralph loses sight of rationality after Piggy is killed and his wisdom is gone. The signal fire represents the hope of rescue and indicates the strength of the boys' connection to civilization. The fire dies when the boys' hope of rescue or their desire to return to civilization wanes. The fire is portrayed as being both helpful and fatal. The boys mainly use it for cooking and rescue, but Jack uses it as a weapon to harm Ralph. A littlun is also most likely killed in the boys' accidental wildfire. The beast is created by the littluns' fear, which represents humankind's fear of the unknown. Later, as the fear of the beast spreads, it represents the primal savagery within all humans. The dead parachutist as the physical beast represents the adults' war and savagery off of the island. The Lord of the Flies, the staked sow's head, symbolizes evil and has the power to communicate with the*

darker side of humans. Other possible symbols include: the scar left by the plane crash, the snake-like imagery, the tide and the sun, butterflies, the platform, the shelters, and the tribal chanting and dancing. The scar represents the encroachment of humanity's destructive forces onto the island, the snake-like imagery may represent aggression or fear, the tide and the sun indicate the passing of time and the orderliness of nature, butterflies show the delicate beauty of nature and may represent innocence and goodness, the platform symbolizes the seat of government while the logs represent Ralph's and Jack's thrones, the shelters symbolize home and security, and the tribal chanting and dancing represent loss of reason.)

9. Some book reviewers do not think *Lord of the Flies* is suitable for classroom use because the novel contains violence. Other reviewers consider the novel a classic and "superbly written." Which reviewers do you agree with, and why? *(Answers will vary. Students should consider that the violence in the novel supports the author's main idea that savagery exists within every human. They should also note that the author's use of imagery and allegorical layers results in a complex story that readers can enjoy on many levels. Each reading of the novel reveals additional depth and is the main reason the novel is considered a classic.)*

10. Evaluate the denouement of *Lord of the Flies*. Was it satisfying, or did it leave you wondering what will happen to the boys next? How do you think events on the island will affect the boys permanently? *(Answers will vary. The conclusion of the novel leaves readers wondering if the boys and the officer will get off the island, what will happen when they get home, how the boys will interact with each other after, and what kinds of issues [mentally, emotionally, and physically] they will have.)*

11. Do you think *Lord of the Flies* is relevant to your life in any way? *(Answers will vary. Discussion should cover identity, conformity, and basic desires. Most students will relate to the story's messages of the need for self-control, taking responsibility for one's actions, and the value of kindness toward and acceptance of others.)*

Post-reading Extension Activities

Writing

1. Write an allegorical short story with the same themes as the novel but with a different setting.

2. Read a copy of R. M. Ballantyne's *The Coral Island*, and compare and contrast it to *Lord of the Flies*.

3. Read William Golding's essay "Why Boys Become Vicious" (available online). Write an essay on whether you agree with Golding. Support your opinion with historical and current events.

4. As a class, create a blog about *Lord of the Flies*. Include analysis and a review of the novel. Design a chart that would be helpful for tracking the novel's themes, symbols, and motifs.

Media

5. With your teacher's permission, play the *Lord of the Flies* game at http://www.nobelprize.org/educational/literature/golding (active at time of publication).

6. Watch the 1963 and 1990 movie versions of *Lord of the Flies*, and then give an oral report comparing and contrasting the movies with the novel. Discuss the characters, setting, plot, events, and themes.

Art

7. Design a three-dimensional map of the island using a medium of your choice (e.g., a clay model or computer program).

8. Design your own cover for the novel. The teacher may choose to hold a classroom competition to determine which student's cover best represents the novel.

9. Create a collage depicting the "goodness" and "evil" of human nature.

Research

10. Design a pamphlet about post-traumatic stress disorder. Provide information that would be helpful to Ralph and the other characters in the novel.

11. Create a video documentary about survival techniques. Discuss ways to meet physical and emotional needs. Support your commentary by creating models and other visual displays.

12. Research Thomas Hobbes', John Locke's, and Jean-Jacques Rousseau's theories on human nature. Then, write an essay explaining which philosopher's theory best describes the conflict in *Lord of the Flies*.

Assessment for *Lord of the Flies*

Assessment is an ongoing process. The following ten items can be completed during the novel study. Once finished, the student and teacher will check the work. Points may be added to indicate the level of understanding.

Name _____ Date _____

Student　　　**Teacher**

_____　　_____　　1. Complete a Character Web (see page 34 of this guide) for both Ralph and Jack. Then, compare and contrast the two characters.

_____　　_____　　2. Choose one of your Allegory charts (from Initiating Activity #4), and share it in class.

_____　　_____　　3. Complete the Conflict chart on page 35 of this guide.

_____　　_____　　4. Select three characters and five symbols from the novel, and write a short essay explaining what each represents in the novel.

_____　　_____　　5. Complete the Rainstorming chart on page 36 of this guide.

_____　　_____　　6. Complete the Story Map on page 37 of this guide.

_____　　_____　　7. Write a poem about using fear to manipulate others.

_____　　_____　　8. Write an essay about human nature based on what you learned from the novel.

_____　　_____　　9. Using the Sorting Characters chart on page 38 of this guide, determine a theme in the novel. Then, discuss with classmates how the theme is developed.

_____　　_____　　10. Correct all quizzes and tests taken over the course of the novel.

I Predict...

Directions: Spend a few minutes looking at the cover of the novel and flipping through its pages. What can you predict about the characters, the setting, and the problem in the novel? Write your predictions in the spaces below.

The Characters	The Setting	The Problem

From the information you gathered above, do you think you will enjoy reading this novel? Circle your response on the scale below.

0 —— 1 —— 2 —— 3 —— 4 —— 5 —— 6 —— 7 —— 8 —— 9 —— 10

I will not like this novel.   I will really like this novel.

Explain your prediction on the lines below.

_____

_____

_____

_____

_____

_____

_____

Allegory

Directions: Use a chart like the one below to analyze each chapter of the novel.

Title of chapter:
After reading this chapter, write a brief summary below.
In the space provided below, list characters, events, and objects that may represent an idea or concept.
Summarize the main idea and significance of the chapter.

Clue Log

Directions: When you read something you think might be important later in the novel, write it down. See if you can predict the novel's ending.

Page	Clue (event or item)	Could have something to do with—

Using Dialogue

Directions: Choose some dialogue from the current reading section. Fill in the chart to evaluate the purpose of the dialogue and whether or not it is effective in moving along the plot.

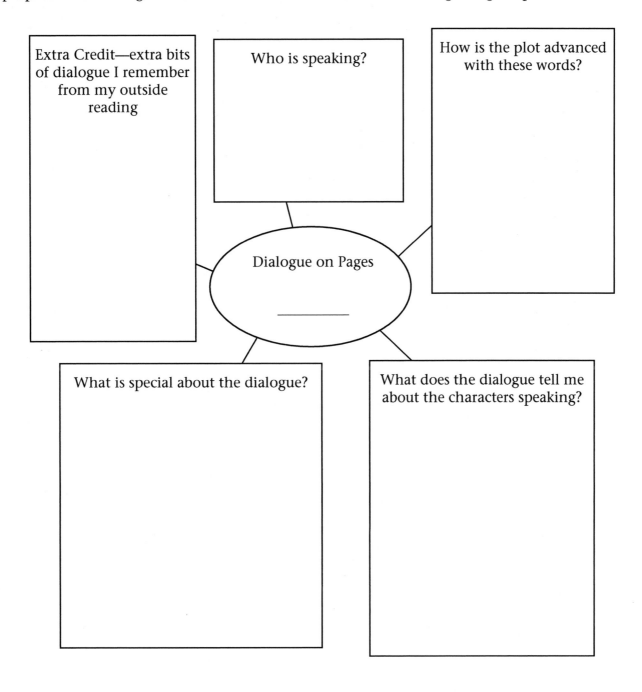

Extra Credit—extra bits of dialogue I remember from my outside reading

Who is speaking?

How is the plot advanced with these words?

Dialogue on Pages

_____

What is special about the dialogue?

What does the dialogue tell me about the characters speaking?

Thought Bubble

Directions: In the graphic below, write what Roger may have been thinking while hunting the beast with Ralph and Jack. Write from Roger's point of view, and include his thoughts on the power struggle between Ralph and Jack.

Think About It

Directions: Use the chart below to answer a question you have about the novel. Provide three reasons and three examples that help answer your question.

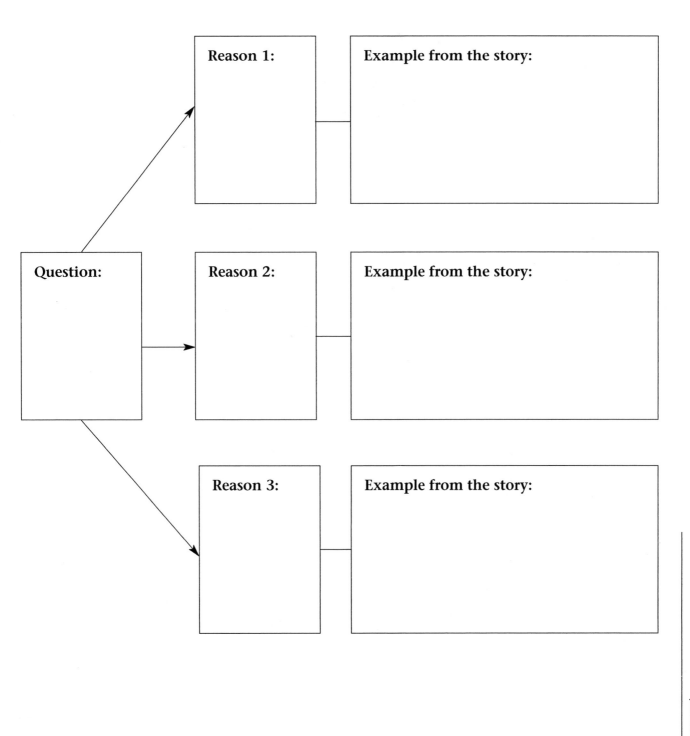

Character Web

Directions: Complete the attribute web below by filling in information specific to Ralph. Then, complete another web for Jack.

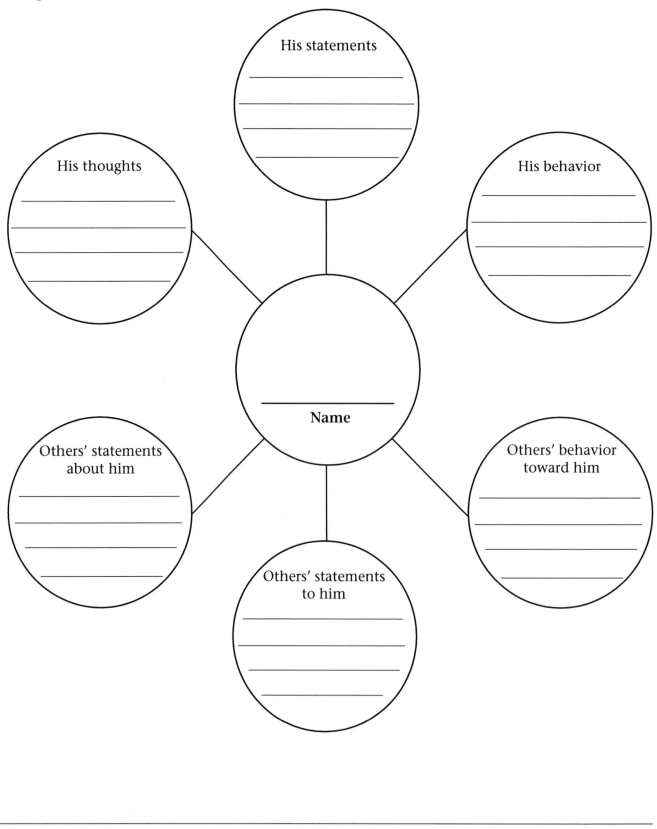

Conflict

The **conflict** of a story is the struggle between two people or two forces. There are four main types of conflict: person vs. person, person vs. nature, person vs. society, and person vs. self.

Directions: In the space provided, list four conflicts a character experiences and justify why you identify it with that particular type of conflict. Then, explain how each conflict is resolved in the story.

person vs. person

Conflict	Resolution

person vs. nature

Conflict	Resolution

person vs. society

Conflict	Resolution

person vs. self

Conflict	Resolution

Rainstorming

Directions: Use the clouds below to track the effects of Jack's obsession with hunting. Use the clouds on the left to show the effects his obsession has on Ralph's group, and use the clouds on the right to show the effects on Jack's tribe.

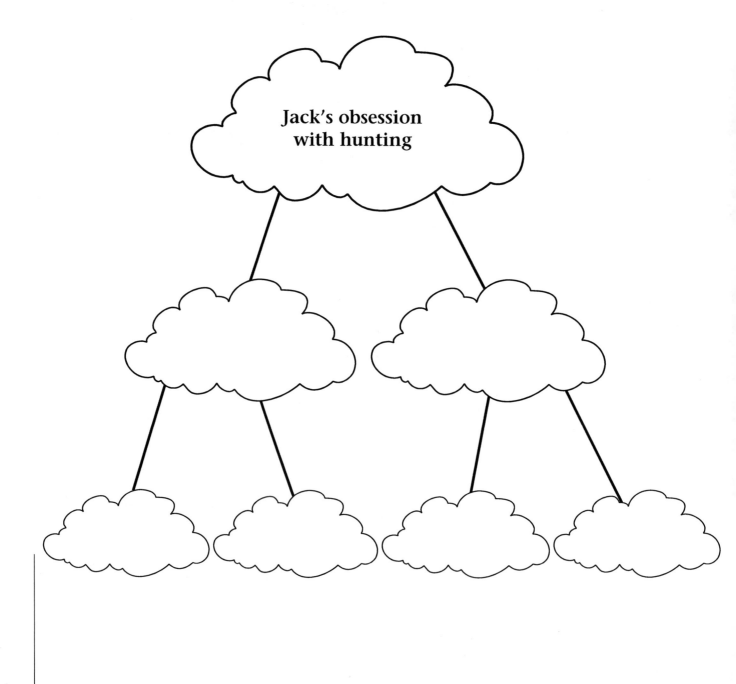

Story Map

Directions: Complete the story map below with information about the novel.

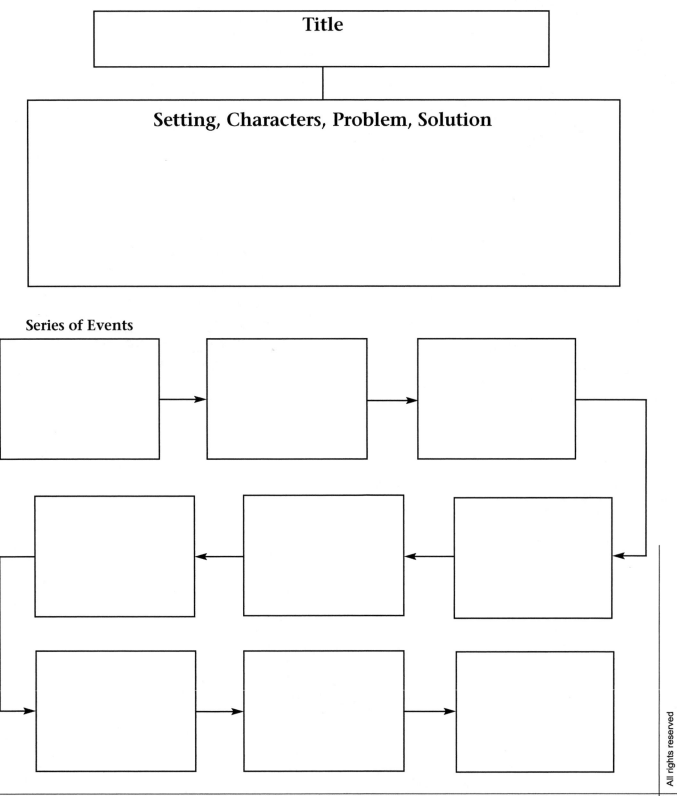

Title

Setting, Characters, Problem, Solution

Series of Events

Sorting Characters

Directions: Similarities between characters are sometimes a clue to themes in a story. Place this novel's characters in one or more of the groups below.

Victims	Victimizers	Fighters
Peace-lovers	**Conformists**	**Self-directors**

Linking Novel Units® Lessons to National and State Reading Assessments

During the past several years, an increasing number of students have faced some form of state-mandated competency testing in reading. Many states now administer state-developed assessments to measure the skills and knowledge emphasized in their particular reading curriculum. The discussion questions and post-reading questions in this Novel Units® Teacher Guide make excellent open-ended comprehension questions and may be used throughout the daily lessons as practice activities. The rubric below provides important information for evaluating responses to open-ended comprehension questions. Teachers may also use scoring rubrics provided for their own state's competency test.

Please note: The Novel Units® Student Packet contains optional open-ended questions in a format similar to many national and state reading assessments.

Scoring Rubric for Open-Ended Items

3-Exemplary	Thorough, complete ideas/information Clear organization throughout Logical reasoning/conclusions Thorough understanding of reading task Accurate, complete response
2-Sufficient	Many relevant ideas/pieces of information Clear organization throughout most of response Minor problems in logical reasoning/conclusions General understanding of reading task Generally accurate and complete response
1-Partially Sufficient	Minimally relevant ideas/information Obvious gaps in organization Obvious problems in logical reasoning/conclusions Minimal understanding of reading task Inaccuracies/incomplete response
0-Insufficient	Irrelevant ideas/information No coherent organization Major problems in logical reasoning/conclusions Little or no understanding of reading task Generally inaccurate/incomplete response

Glossary

Chapters One–Two

adj 1. effulgence: radiance *(14)*

n. 2. enmity: hostility; animosity *(14)*

✓ 3. interposed: intervened; interfered *(16)*

adj 4. strident: loud; harsh *(17)*

adj 5. furtive: sly; secretive *(22)* *(-Roger)*

✓ 6. suffusion: spread of color

n. 7. pallor: paleness; lack of color

n. 8. indignation: anger at something unreasonable or unfair

v 9. immured: imprisoned; enclosed; surrounded

n 10. hiatus: unexpected break in continuity

✓ 11. gesticulated: made animated or excited gestures

n 12. ebullience: enthusiasm; exhilaration; high spirits

adj 13. grotesque: odd or unnatural in shape

adj 14. officious: aggressive in giving one's unwanted help; meddlesome

n 15. recrimination: retaliatory charge against an accuser

n 16. realism: view of circumstances as they really are

n 17. tumult: noisy commotion of a crowd; disorder

n 18. tirade: prolonged outburst of bitter denunciation

Chapters Three–Four

1. festooned: adorned; decorated
2. tendril: threadlike, leafless part of a climbing plant
3. inscrutable: incapable of being analyzed; unfathomable
4. vicissitudes: regular changes in nature
5. compulsion: obsession; obligation
6. opaque: not clear or lucid; obscure
7. declivities: downward slopes
8. tacit: understood without being openly expressed; implied
9. susurration: soft murmur; whisper
10. blatant: shamelessly obvious; flagrant
11. dubious: questionable; doubtful
12. belligerence: aggressively hostile nature
13. chastisement: punishment; severe criticism

14. impalpable: incapable of being perceived by touch; intangible

15. detritus: disintegrated material; debris

16. preposterous: absurd; contrary to reason

17. swarthiness: dark tone

18. disinclination: reluctance; unwillingness

19. implications: suggestions that aren't explicitly stated

20. malevolently: dishonorably; maliciously

Chapters Five–Six

1. convulsion: extreme disruption or disturbance

2. ludicrous: ridiculous; laughable

3. derisive: mocking; contemptuous

4. effigy: representation; image

5. lamentation: grief; wailing

6. decorum: dignified behavior

7. inarticulate: unable to express oneself

8. tempestuously: violently; tumultuously

9. discursive: wandering; rambling

10. theorem: theoretical proposition

11. incantation: recited formula of words designed to produce a particular effect

12. taut: tightly drawn

13. interminable: unending

14. tremulously: shakily; quaveringly; unsteadily

15. emphatic: uttered with emphasis; strongly expressed

16. embroiled: involved in conflict

17. diffidently: timidly; shyly

18. plinth: square base or lower block of a pedestal

Chapters Seven–Eight

1. coverts: shelters; hiding places

2. obtuseness: dimness; denseness

3. vulnerable: capable of being wounded; susceptible

4. luxuriance: rich abundance

5. traverses: places to cross

6. sagely: judiciously; wisely

7. impervious: unaffected; not capable of being disturbed

8. bravado: display of courage or boldness

9. rebuke: express stern disproval; reprimand

10. demure: reserved; shy

11. fervor: earnestness of feeling; intensity

12. cynicism: bitterness; distrust

13. obscene: indecent; morally offensive

14. illusive: deceptive; unreal

15. runnels: small channels; gutters

16. vexed: irritated; troubled

17. parody: feeble imitation; travesty

Chapters Nine–Ten

1. corpulent: large or bulky of body; stout

2. succulent: lush; tasty

3. sauntered: walked leisurely; strolled

4. demented: crazy; insane

5. superficial: of little substance

6. complementary: that which completes or benefits something else

7. abominable: unpleasant; hateful

8. phosphorescence: bright in appearance

9. inquisitive: eager for knowledge; intellectually curious

10. befouled: defiled; sullied; dirtied

11. somberly: seriously; gravely

12. torrid: oppressively hot

13. assimilating: thoroughly comprehending

14. interrogative: questioning

15. theological: pertaining to a religious theory or system of belief

16. purged: rid of something undesirable; purified

Chapters Eleven–Twelve

1. luminous: reflecting light; bright
2. myopia: lack of discernment
3. propitiatingly: appeasingly; favorably
4. vitality: abundant energy combined with a joyous approach to life
5. quavered: trembled; uttered fearfully
6. truculently: with aggressive hostility; savagely
7. anonymity: lack of distinctive features and individuality
8. cessation: discontinuation; ceasing
9. parried: averted; dodged
10. talisman: object which exercises powerful influence
11. inimical: unfriendly; hostile
12. ululation: howl; wail
13. ensconce: shelter; hide securely
14. cordon: line of soldiers guarding an area
15. crepitation: crackling sound
16. excruciatingly: painfully; agonizingly
17. epaulettes: ornamental shoulder pieces worn on military uniforms
18. distended: swollen by internal pressure

Notes